Gallery Books
Editor: Peter Fallon

THE PRINCE OF THE QUOTIDIAN

Paul Muldoon

THE PRINCE
OF THE
QUOTIDIAN

Gallery Books

The Prince of the Quotidian
was first published
simultaneously in paperback
and in a clothbound edition
on 22 July 1994.

The Gallery Press
Loughcrew
Oldcastle
County Meath
Ireland

ISBN 1 85235 137 3 (*paperback*)
    1 85235 138 1 (*clothbound*)

The Gallery Press receives financial assistance from An Chomhairle
Ealaíon / The Arts Council, Ireland, and acknowledges also the assistance of The Arts Council of Northern Ireland in the publication of
this book.

THE PRINCE
OF THE
QUOTIDIAN

I moved in consequence my family to Princeton, where I hired a small house for the winter, which I furnished frugally but decently. I fitted up my study and began to think my lot was cast to be an American farmer.

— Theobald Wolfe Tone to Thomas Russell, 1795

After breakfast with Belinda and Philip Haas
we stowed their bassinet
in the trunk
and struck out for the Holland Tunnel.

The lights were all against us.
A man with a belly like a poisoned
pup careened towards us, much the worse for drink.
Another lurched from a Tenniel

with a squeegee and a squirt
of blue. Yet another wore a caul
made from a beach-towel edged with a blue flower;

'Try,' he said, 'try not to confuse *carrus*, a cart,
with *carina*, a keel . . . '
The light turned green. I put my foot to the floor.

A native New Yorker, Jean thinks it nothing short of heresy
that I might respond to a questionnaire
from *Who's Who in New Jersey*;
has she forgotten Zabinski, cut down in a barber's chair

in Brooklyn or darkest Queens?
I bring this up over dinner at George Pitcher and Ed Cone's.

The more I think of it, the more I've come to love
the tidal marshes of Hackensack,
the planes stacked
over Newark, even the smell of cloves

and chloroform
that sweetens Elizabeth.
(At Exit 9, the man in the toll-booth
almost lost an arm

to Oscar Mac Oscar, as we call the hound . . . .)
The more I think of it, the less I'm clear
as to why U2 should spend a year
remaking themselves as a garage band.

Which reminds me; we must see the new Wim Wenders.
In the meantime, let's rent *Pathfinder*.

The mail brings 'literature' from Louisiana
on various plantation tours
and a Christmas poem from Doctor Heaney:

the great physician of the earth
is waxing metaphysical, has taken to 'walking on air';
as Goethe termed it, *Surf und Turf.*

Through Washington Crossing, New Hope, Lambertville,
we putter along the Delaware
with Louis and Louise. In a store filled
with Depression glass and Fiestaware

I come on a postcard of the Empire State
and the legend
in a bold copperplate;
'I'll be waiting on Tuesday at Broadway and 52nd.'

Louise confirms what Jean has already guessed;
something has sickened
and died under the dining-room floor. The Volvo wagon,
meanwhile, is about to give up the ghost.

This slow air played on the ocarina
is a lament for my long-lost cousin, Marina.

A Twelfth Night bash with Mimi and Larry Danson
and most of the Princeton heavy
hitters: 'Mike' Keeley, Constantine Cavafy,

Elaine Showalter
and Oscar Wilde rub shoulders
with Russell Banks and Arnold Rampersad;

I insert myself like an ampersand
between Joyce Carol Oates & Ingemar Johansson.

The Feast of the Epiphany. It's been so mild
the bell of millet
strung up for the finches
is all but dumb: a few inches

of snow, one hard frost,
might draw the deer out of the forest
to prune the vines
from the picket fence

or vault the five-foot chicken-wire cordon
round our herb-garden.
In the meantime, my lemon-peel

and bacon-rind mobile
is losing something of its verve.
I wait in vain for some small showing forth.

I get myself up in black tie and monkey-suit
and follow the glittering path
to the Met for *The Ghosts
of Versailles*, an opera so terminally *bouffe*

even the Montgolfiers' hot-air balloon
seems a leaden leitmotif —
'Where's the bouillon,
never mind the beef?'

During the interval, I fortify myself
with a meringue.
I run into George and Ed, but not Daron Hagen:

I've written some new lines for The Chef
in the style of Amergin;
these I declaim to the burghers of Weehawken.

Weehawken. Kearny. The Oranges. I'm filled with dismay
by news of two murders in The Moy.

Little did I think that when I gave her *Time's Arrow*
Jean would give me a blue wheelbarrow
on which so mulch, so very mulch
depends. Julie Agoos is back from the MLA

with greetings from 'Coleslaw' Milosz,
Dillon, and Guinn, who delivered a brief homily
on my 'cauliflower' period: would that I were the Amadeus
of carrots and parsnips, scallions and tomatoes.

Only a few weeks ago, the sonogram of Jean's womb
resembled nothing so much
as a satellite map of Ireland:

now the image
is so well-defined we can make out not only a hand
but a thumb;

on the road to Spiddal, a woman hitching a ride;
a gladiator in his net, passing judgement on the crowd.

The last time I saw *Three Sisters*
was in a 'vershin' by Monsignor Friel, who was,
I recall, at pains to prove that Chekhov was more Irish
than a rush:

why should 'Field Day' continue to peddle
its 'old whines in new bottles?'
Why should this band of balladeers and bards
add up to so much less than the sum of its parts

like almost every Irish stew?
If only we knew . . . If only we knew
how Renée and Ted Weiss
will get on with our other dinner guests, the Listers.

I open the freezer. The blood-besmirched
face of Kevin McKearney
implores me from a hospital gurney;
'Won't you at least visit my grave in March?'

After two days grading papers from the seminar I taught
on Swift, Yeats, Sterne,
Joyce, and Beckett,
I break my sword across my iron knee:

in the long sonata of *The Dead*
ceremony's a name for the rich horn —
these images fresh images beget —
and custom for the hardy laurel tree;

for the gravel was thrown up against the window-pane
not by Michael Furey but the Dean
who stepped on to an outward bound tram

and embarked on *Immram Curaig Mael Duin*,
while the Butler that withstood beside the brackish Boyne
was one James Butler, Corporal Trim.

That man with the belly like a poisoned pup
was once a strange child with a taste for verse:
now everything turns on a pub;
'The Lion's Head', 'McKenna's', 'The White Horse'.

As we zoomed past Loyola and Tulane
I could think only of my nephew, Dillon,
born two days ago in Canada.
'Let him,' I heard, 'let him be one ignited by the quaint

in this new quotidian: a mound
of coffee beans in the 'Café du Monde';
the New Orleans School of Cookery's
okra-

monious gumbo; a dirigible of Paul Prudhomme
floating above the Superdome;
let the Prince of the Quotidian lead an alligator

along the *banquette* of Decatur
yet let him not, with Alejandro O'Reilly,
forget the cries of the bittern and the curlew.'

An alley of live oaks festooned with Spanish moss
ran from the levee
flanking the Mississippi
to the Greek Revival plantation house at Houmas:

the Aquarium's
shoal of piranhas,
the whiff from Pat O'Brien's
thousand and one rums,

the Museum of Voodoo's
shrine to Marie Laveau —
all had faded beside that sepia . . .
that 'sepia photo'

of the slave quarters; a girl-child with a mussel-spoon;
we cancelled our reservation at 'Bayona'.

Old Satchmo breathed on 'Eddie's' oyster loaf
and blessed and broke it; 'What we play is life.'

Not for nothing would I versify
'The Alchemist and Barrister', rhyme (*pace* Longley) 'cat'
with 'dog', expand on the forsythia
that graces our back door: 'humdrum', 'inadequate',

'inconsequential journalese', 'a klieg light
masquerading as the moon'; none will,
I trust, look for a pattern in this crazy quilt
where all is random, 'all so trivial',

unless it be Erasmus, unless
Erasmus again steel
himself as his viscera are cranked out by a windlass

yard upon 'xanthous' yard;
again to steel himself, then somehow to exhort
the windlass-men to even greater zeal.

We followed Lafitte and the great McIlhenny
and all that pirate krewe
on a flat-boat through Honey
Island swamp in search of the *loup garou*.

We saw a heron, an egret,
and the nest of a bald eagle
whose stance, John Burnside argued,
was strictly apolitical.

So we fell upon the heron, a hapless goose,
and a shoulder
of wild boar: these would sustain us until

we sat down with Frances Parkinson Keyes
for a farewell dinner of crawfish and andouille
not at 'Antoine's' but 'Galatoire's'.

Despite the fact that it's now considerably colder
and there's even some snow on the ground
my Alexander Calder
still gleams with gobbets of pork-rind . . . .

'Gobbets of pork-rind'? A moment later I see
them 'hung . . . on our eight-foot magnolia tree . . . '

Our magnolia's overwhelmed by a honey locust
just as I am, I suppose,
by this sprawling, self-invited guest
and his amniotic vodka with a dash of 'Old Spice'.

I was standing with Oliver Stone by the grassy knoll
trying to find an angle on *The Saga of Burnt Njal*.

That our child's due date is the Twelfth of July —
the anniversary of the birth of Neruda
but a red-letter day in El Norte
rather than Chile —

is an irony that won't escape
the 'Longalley' or the famous 'Montagael':
I spend the evening transferring the new Lloyd Cole
and *Cajun Classics* from CD to tape.

By the time I've reached the Delaware Water Gap
it's already seven
and I take a break from Warren Zevon
for 'a great big dish' of scrapple and a cup

of coffee. The moon hangs over the Poconos
like a madeleine.
Warren Zevon. 'Van the Man'. Bob Dylan.
At Scranton I toil in the wake of two canoes

against a river of anthracite. It's almost ten
when I check into the 'Hotel
de Ville' in Binghamton

where half the Arts Council and umpteen
ex-colleagues from the BBC huddle
in the bar with a dozen off-duty windlass-men.

Much as I'm taken by Barry Douglas playing Rachmaninov
with the Ulster Orchestra
I remember why I've had enough
of the casuistry

by which pianists and painters and poets are proof
that all's not rotten in the state:
amid the cheers and the cries of 'Bravo'
I hear the howls of seven dead

at a crossroads between Omagh and long Cookstown.
The 'trivial' happens where 'three roads' meet.
Does Saint Augustine

'trivialise' the sack of Rome?
I sit up late in Longley's little room
and listen to him conjugate, '*Amayo, amayas, amayat* . . . . '

Snow on the ground. The narcissi
nipped in the bud. In the latest issue
of the *TLS* 'the other Seamus', Seamus Deane,

has me 'in exile' in Princeton:
this term serves mostly to belittle
the likes of Brodsky or Padilla

and is not appropriate of me; certainly not
of anyone who, with 'Louisa May' Walcott,
is free to buy a ticket to his emerald isle

of choice. To Deane I say, 'I'm not "in exile",
though I can't deny
that I've been twice in Fintona.'

It seems that yesterday I let off so much steam
the snow melted and a small green
finch — it was a goldfinch, I dare say —
perched on the haft
of the snow-shovel and began to preen;

'I who looked over the shoulders of Mandelstam
and your friends Bob Tracy
and Clarence Brown
remind you now as I reminded Ovid:
try not to confuse your "*cor*" with your "Corinna".'

As I coasted into the tunnel
of the Pennington car wash
I glanced at my copy of *Feis*
by Nuala Ní Dhomhnaill:

a wave broke over a rock
somewhere west of Dingle;
my windshield was a tangle
of eel-grass and bladderwrack.

Six o'clock. Jean and I have snuggled up on the sofa
to watch Jim Jarmusch's *Mystery Train*
when Medbh calls: I can barely refrain
from letting slip that it's 'Aoife . . . Dorothy Aoife . . . . '

I look out the kitchen window. A cigarette burns
in the midst of the pyracanthus:
'What's with you, *a mhic*?
Apart from the 'eel-grass and bladderwrack'

there's not an image here that's worth a fuck.
Who gives a shit about the dreck
of your life? Who gives a toss
about your tossing off?' 'I know, I know, but . . . '

'But nothing: you know it's dross;
you know that 'Erasmus' stuff is an inept
attempt to cover your arse;

leave off your laundry-lists and tax-returns
and go back to making metaphors . . . . '
Something in that 'go back' reminds me of Xanthus.

With that the horse-head folds his horse-hide parachute
till it's no bigger than a glove:

he slaps my cheek; 'Above all else, you must atone
for everything you've said and done

against your mother: meet excess of love
with excess of love; begin on the Feast of Saint Brigid.'